awakening
the
miracle
OF
YOU

AFFIRMATIONS FOR YOUR LIFE

JUDITH COLLINS

hachette
AUSTRALIA

hachette
AUSTRALIA

This edition published in Australia and New Zealand in 2017
by Hachette Australia
(an imprint of Hachette Australia Pty Limited)
Level 17, 207 Kent Street, Sydney NSW 2000
www.hachette.com.au

The authorised representative
in the EEA is
Hachette Ireland
8 Castlecourt Centre
Dublin 15, D15 XTP3, Ireland
(email: info@hbgi.ie)

First published as *Affirmations* for Life in 1997 by Thomas C Lothian Pty Ltd

10 9 8 7 6 5 4 3 2

National Library of Australia
Cataloguing-in-Publication data:

Collins, Judith, author.

Awakening the miracle of you/Judith Collins.

ISBN: 978 0 7336 3669 1 (paperback)

Affirmations.
Mindfulness (Psychology)
Self-help techniques.
Self-consciousness (Awareness)
Mind and body.

158.1

Cover design by Christabella Designs
Cover image courtesy of Shutterstock
Internal image courtesy of iStock
Text design by Kirby Jones
Typeset in Helvetical Neue LT Std by Kirby Jones
Printed and bound in Great Britain by Clays Ltd, Elcograf S.p.A.

MIX
Paper | Supporting
responsible forestry
FSC
www.fsc.org **FSC® C104740**

To the memory of my loving grandmother, Margaret Anne Kensey, who believed throughout her life that every cloud has a silver lining and who took the time to instil her belief in a young and impressionable me.

And to the memory of my cousin David who forgot what our grandmother taught us.

A SPECIAL THANK YOU

I wish to extend my heartfelt thanks to a mysterious woman in her mid-80s, whom I came across in Melbourne in 1996. She politely interrupted a conversation I was having with a friend and asked to borrow a pen so that she could write me a note. 'This is for you, my dear,' she said, slipping the folded note securely into my hand and gripping it tightly for a second. And this is what she wrote …

I can be anything I choose
That's the most important news.
Though there be those of other views,
It's I that, nonetheless, doth choose.

To my amazement, two days later I was approached to write this book. Some hours were spent in solitude evaluating the message as it had also come at a time when I was being pulled in all directions by public demand and needed to take a firm hold on my life. But how did she know?

Contents

INTRODUCTION

As I recall, I was six years of age when I made my first affirmation in an announcement to my school friends: 'I'll be a writer when I grow up.' I never lost sight of this goal all of my life. At the age of six years my friend, Fr Justin Belitz, a Franciscan friar and author of the book *Success: Full Living*, heard the story of St Francis of Assisi and immediately affirmed to himself and family that he would follow in the steps of St Francis. Another close friend affirmed at twelve years of age that she would be wealthy; she married a successful businessman who in later years inherited the family estate.

After the completion of his now world famous book *The Power of Positive Thinking*, Norman Vincent Peale had great difficulty finding a publisher for his work. But for his total confidence in his work, affirming its worth, this bestseller may have never been read by anyone except family and friends.

Coincidence? Not at all. You may think that these people were strong willed, even relentless in their pursuits. Nothing could be further from the truth. Life didn't do any of them special favours. It is attitude, the choices we make and the strength of our desires that allow us to achieve the goals we set.

The power of the mind, alone, does not guarantee the success of a desired goal. Some action is required to prove your commitment and intention. When thought and effort are combined, the conscious mind is well on the way to being convinced that a reality is being created and that achievement is in sight. Just sitting back and wishing rarely gets the desired result. I know this first hand.

I awoke one morning to find that both my legs and my left arm were paralysed. Countless tests and visits to medical specialists and hospitals did not identify the cause. To frustrate the situation further my body did not respond to any treatment. It was an anxious time when I was told I would probably never walk again.

My husband was studying engineering at university full time and I was the sole source of income. We had only been married six months, and financially we were struggling. In a distraught moment I remember telling him to leave me, suggesting I would only be an anchor around his neck in my condition. And, really, that's the last thing I needed.

For endless boring hours I lay on my back in our little caravan home, trying to annihilate time. I had nothing to do but think and read, read and think. For ten hours every day the only conversation I had was with insects or myself. I devised a game of mentally dividing my body into halves, one representing good health, the other disabled. Then, I proceeded to question them. One day I asked the right side of my body if it was a quitter or a fighter. As my body slowly explained that nothing was preventing it from healing, and that it was just waiting for the appropriate healing method, I began to gain hope. From that moment on, I repeated aloud, 'Whatever will fix me, show yourself now'.

Two weeks later my mother was visiting her optometrist, a family acquaintance, to have her glasses fixed. Bringing him up to date with the family news, I became a major topic of conversation. Just as well! He told her of a very talented chiropractor who had helped him. Mum thought it worth a try and hurriedly made an appointment for me.

Late that afternoon my husband carried me into the chiropractor's clinic, accompanied by my mother for moral support. Seeing me, the chiropractor rescheduled his appointments, and for the next two and a quarter hours worked on me. First he tried osteopathy, then some chiropractic moves. At intervals he paused to monitor my progress by iridology through reading my eyes. Finally he tried a therapy he had learnt in America some months earlier, using a machine that fed sound waves along the spine and the muscles. To our surprise I began to move my toes slightly. As he worked longer and more intensely, my legs responded too.

Standing me upright beside him for support, we walked around and around his desk, working the muscles gently but firmly. Then, he flung the door open and walked me out to the waiting room, where my husband and mother were seated. I'll never forget the spontaneous, joyful tears they shed in celebration of my release from disablement.

The healing of my ailment proved to be a catalyst in changing the entire family's thinking about natural health, as they watched my progress over the next year. For my part, I had learned that the power of my mind was amazing and I could apply it to anything I wanted. A year later I hung up my walking stick.

Courage and strength are often gained by both observers and participants in a tragedy. My husband had to work every night and alternate weekends to feed us, while also coping with his university course and a crippled wife at home in bed and with no hope for the future. 'All character-building experiences,' he says, looking back at that time.

Just as the mind can work for you, it can also work against you through negative programming. Unintentionally, most adults handicap their children by instilling their own personal fears in them and by providing negative long-range forecasts such as, 'You'll never amount to anything' or 'High blood pressure is a fact of life in this family'. An adult who has been schooled in this way as a child tends to reflect his or her parents' fears or to reject them outwardly.

Habits, thought patterns and behaviour can be passed from generation to generation until someone has the courage and determination to cause a change. For instance, a friend whose family had a history of high blood pressure instituted a diet and lifestyle which finally broke the chain in the family's medical history.

When I was growing up, my mother never allowed me to have an umbrella because she said I would lose it, so when I started work as a teenager I immediately bought an umbrella.

Mum's umbrella losses over the years total several; mine total none. You don't need to wear your childhood baggage.

Fortunately I grew up in a well-balanced, caring family where negative programming was minimal. A favourite family put-down is, 'Don't forget you're working class.' To me this aims to restrict your ability to rise above your station; definitely not indicative of more progressive times.

How you respond to life as it dishes out its several-course menu of delights and disasters depends entirely on your attitude and belief systems. Both can be altered to free you up from restrictive life practices.

Life has taught me to take hold of negative experience and transform it to work positively for and not against me. By doing this I exhibit a willingness to release the root cause and consequently life progresses.

My husband and I believe something that started for us as a young romantic gesture over forty years ago is a contributing factor to the daily loving bliss we share. Just before we fall asleep at night, we gently hold hands and whisper, 'As we lay ourselves to sleep, we unite our souls for keep. Wake us now or wake us never, we wish to be together forever and ever.'

When you combine the power of love with the power of the mind there is no telling what you can achieve. Varying degrees of emotional baggage are within us all. But there is also hope and inner friendship. Hope has the power to achieve and also the power to break down barriers and lead us forward. Self-friendship may criticise and take us to task but it also offers support, guidance, forgiveness, understanding, love and loyalty.

I challenge you to be resourceful. Look and feel within. Prove to yourself that you can make a positive difference in your own life.

Humankind is an amazingly adaptable species. Some people have incredible intellects while others can climb mountains, or scale the height of a mature palm tree barefoot in minutes.

Whatever you need to achieve is worth the inner journey. Let the power of hope and self-friendship fill your heart and mind. And begin what you need to do.

AFFIRMATION TECHNIQUES

Time: For optimum results, use affirmations on waking in the morning or just before you go to sleep. During the day the affirmation is best committed to the mind following a relaxed period, or immediately after a meditation, to take advantage of the calmness of the mind.

Place: Create a quiet space at home, at work, or in your mind by restricting your mind's focus on the noise about you.

Method: Steady your breathing to a quiet, easy pace. Repeat your affirmation aloud, meaningfully and with devotion, developing a rhythm in the voice to still the mind's activity and focus. Soften your tone each time you utter the affirmation, more and more quietly, until it fades into a whisper and into a quiet, still thought. Be still for a few moments, feeling and absorbing the affirmation with all of your senses.

TEN STEPS TO CREATING A SUCCESSFUL SELF

This is a guide that I give to my clients to help them evaluate their journey in life.

1. Look deep into your eyes to see the beauty of your soul, a beauty that cannot be scarred or taken from you.

2. Examine your health to identify clearly the state of your mind.

3. Prosperity flourishes with the harnessing of the mind. It is one of the keys to success.

4. Recognise all disappointments as lessons preparing you for future life encounters. Recognise challenges as the yardstick with which you measure your personal growth and values.

5. Listen to your inner voice. It is your intuition speaking.

6. You are purposeful. All experience is purposeful. Each experience perfectly fits into the unfolding pattern of your life.

7. Your soul has a goal to master in this lifetime. Create opportunities for it to excel.

8. Know that you are never alone – a guiding force is within and without you.

9. You will find many friends as you travel life's highways because you originate from a large communion of souls.

10. Know that the greater part of you is spirit – be humble.

USING THIS BOOK

If you have not used affirmations in your life before, you may wish to start with the 52-week course, 'Awakening the Miracle of You'. However, this is not essential and if you know that you need support on a specific matter, use the contents page to find the right affirmation.

You can also weave these individual affirmations into your 52-week course, as needed.

AFFIRMING MUSIC

Music comes to a composer in moments of great inspiration, as do the lyrics which often accompany it. Some composers dedicate themselves to addressing causes through their music, so music is appropriate to use as a support to your affirmations. A recording of an appropriate music compilation can be played at home, in the car or during routine exercise.

When I was twelve years old I came across a composer-singer whose songs of peace, love and happiness sought to guide his audience to evolve as balanced human beings. A girlfriend's seaman cousin was visiting her home and had with him music bought in Europe – names and sounds not yet heard or released in Australia because in the early 1960s we were several years behind the musical advancement of the western world.

Titles like 'Wear your love like heaven' and 'Make up your mind to be happy' attracted me to Donovan who, for more than forty years, has been a creative support to my evolvement. In his song 'Happiness runs' Donovan gives insight into the cycles of happiness and the essence of our spiritual being. He suggests that when you let yourself 'Be' (at peace) you can have everything, a philosophy that has worked for me over the years.

Within weeks of the first publication of this book a journalist planned for our paths to cross. Unbeknown to me Donovan was in Australia. She encouraged him to call me. And he did. We lunched together in a Sydney hotel and then talked for hours. On returning to my car, the whole event emotionally overwhelmed me. I sat stunned as I processed it in my mind.

In the weeks that followed life returned to normal. However, several months later, life became even more inspiring. Donovan called to ask if his dear friend who was in need of convalescence and inspiration could visit me for six weeks. I agreed. Three months after the call, I experienced the thrill of welcoming Lionel Bart, composer and creative genius behind the internationally acclaimed musical production *Oliver!* – an adaptation of *Oliver Twist* by Charles Dickens. It is the tale of a young boy who journeys from the darkness of imposed poverty and petty crime to the resourcefulness of family unity and love.

Music definitely creates a mood. If you are a music lover like myself, you will find that music does half the affirmative work for you. For hours on end and in just about every type of function, I am locked into positive, musical affirmations. One of my favourites for clearing chaotic situations and encouraging me to understand the situation more clearly is the hit song 'I can see clearly now', sung by Jimmy Cliff. It is so inspirational that it was used as the theme song for the motion picture *Cool Runnings*.

Positive words of encouragement which determine a specific line of thinking are essential for attunement of the mind's senses. Affirmative music can send the message to all levels of your senses. Why not make up a playlist?

It is vitally important to avoid music and lyrics which encourage a 'woe-is-me' feeling, because this type of music discourages emotional and mental progress.

awakening
the
miracle
OF
YOU

A FIFTY-TWO WEEK PROGRAMME FOR SELF-DEVELOPMENT AND SELF-AWARENESS

Some years ago I awoke from a deep sleep with the following fifty-two affirmations etched into my memory. They haunted me all through the day until, finally, I recorded them on my computer. In 1995 they were read aloud by a group of actors at a gathering for world peace. The audience was spellbound as each affirmation resonated with the part of them that searched for wholeness.

I understand these affirmations to have been given to me as a gift from a divine source for the sole purpose of encouraging humanity to awaken to the miracle of being fully alive. Their power lies in creating a wholeness of the self by bringing the richness of being human into perspective. Each affirmation is repeated reverently as a prayer, once daily for a period of seven days.

This divinely inspired self-awareness and self-development programme has proven its ability to improve the lives of those who undertake it with reverence and devotion. It takes you through a 52-week term, causing evolution of attitude, intention and feeling. The year-long period provides an excellent yardstick to evaluate your progress.

You can start this course at any point in a calendar year. Trust that you will know the right time.

I walk the path of new beginnings

I know that whatever may come to an end will be the creation of a new beginning.

I place my destiny in the path of my soul.
I welcome the new.

I walk the path of self-acceptance

I realise I am who I need to be.
I realise I do what I need to do.
I realise I feel what I need to feel.
I realise I attract what I need to learn.
I realise I hear what I need to know.
I realise I see what I am to witness.
In this, I deepen my sense of self.

I walk the path of forgiveness

I forgive myself for thoughts and words spoken ill of others.
I forgive others for not hearing nor caring for me.
I forgive my indifference, hesitations and reservations.
I forgive my imbalance.
I forgive, for it is the blessing of the soul.

I walk the path of love

I understand that love is the essence of my existence.

I understand that love embraces my all.

I understand that love links the world and all its inhabitants together.

I accept the love of myself.

I walk the path of hope

I know that hope inspires me to grow.
I know that hope encourages me to welcome
the unfolding of each day.
I accept the creativity of hope, with its images
or advancement.

I walk the path of trust

My decisions are a reflection of my learning.
My actions are a reflection of my learning.
My responses are a reflection of my growth.
I place my trust in my Soul and Spirit to guide
me to total evolvement.

I am the creator of my evolvement

I recognise choices as my own.
I recognise deeds as my own.
My decisions are all purposeful for my learning.

I am a mirror of my learning

All experience is for my progress.
I am a student of life.
I listen to my experience.
I learn from my experience.

I am a purpose within a purpose

My life is the design of Spirit.
Everything I encounter is beneficial to my evolvement.
My mind may not comprehend my learning but my soul is always aware.
My purpose is to accept all experience.

My life is an unfolding flow of self-realisation

Each day I am reborn.
Each day I am charged with the grace of Spirit.
Each day offers a new beginning.
Each day offers the continuation of evolvement.
Each day I measure my personal advancement.

Life experience is a measure of my growth

I recognise that there are no problems in life, only challenges.
I recognise my challenges as a need to master my learning.
In this I witness the advancement of my soul.

Memories are a reflection of my advancement

I think of how I used to think.
I think of how I used to feel.
I think of what I used to know.
I think of how I used to be.
Memories flow, highlighting my progress.

I am an explorer

In the patterns of my learning I chart and travel
my path of self-discovery.
I freely alter my direction when the path ahead
restricts the evolvement of my soul.
I signpost my achievements with experience.

I am an observer

I evolve through sharing the experiences of my
fellow human beings.
My observation is a tool of learning for my
soul.

I am a thinker

My thoughts register within my Mind, Body
and Soul.
Each thought represents my feelings and my
beliefs.
My thoughts evolve to create my reality.

I am a leader

I am responsible for my reality.
I choose my own direction.
In this, I lead my own evolvement.

I am a follower

As I learn and evolve in Spirit I know Divine Inspiration is the force that guides my every step.
I follow where I am led for my soul to unfold in the glory of the great Spirit.

I am a healer

From within me stems the energy to heal my wounds.

When I self-heal, I truly witness the grace of my soul.

In healing myself, I grow in recognition of myself.

I am a communicator

My words are an expression of my innermost convictions.
I choose them carefully so as to express the balance of who I have chosen to be.

I am a negotiator

I discuss. I do not debate.
I reason. I do not argue.
I learn while I listen.
I value all opinion as learning.

I do not judge others

I see life as a lesson for everyone.
Choices are the steps of learning.
All experience is chosen for personal
evolvement.

I am a messenger of light

I am open to inspiration from the Divine Spirit.
I welcome the light. I bathe myself in the light.

I am a missionary

I spread light in the path of others.
I spread enlightenment in all conversations.
I preach togetherness in all things.
In this, I am serving the Divine Spirit.

I am a compassionate soul

My soul has come to life to serve others and to expand my gift of charity.

I am a torch

I increase the light of my soul for my soul's direction.
As I expand in spirit I shine my light for others to follow.

I am charity

My soul teaches and learns compassion.
I am spontaneously kind to others.
I help where help is needed.
In my kindness, I am blessed.

I am a peacemaker

My soul is a vessel of peace.
My mind seeks peace.
Together they rejoice in spreading peace
within me.

I am a believer

I expand my knowing in every waking moment
of the day.
My beliefs unfold at the pace of my chosen
learning.

I am strong

My direction is the path of my soul's learning.
My thoughts are the navigation skills of my
soul's learning.
My feelings are the lessons of my soul's
learning.

I am rich

My soul is an abundance of grace.
I attract the appropriate level of prosperity for my learning.
My wealth stems from my self-awareness.

I am beautiful

Created in the perfection of my soul's learning,
I accept who I am as the path of my evolution
unfolds.

I am perfect in every way

I accept who I am and what I am, for I realise my purpose is to grow in perfection here on earth and to live in spirit.

Each day the perfection of self unfolds.

I am love

My soul is a mirror image of the Divine Spirit.
I feel my connection to love.
I grow through love.
My path is love.

I am expression

I expand with thought.
I expand with feeling.
I expand with deed.
I am creation within creation, unfolding as
I express my being on Earth.

I am a singer of life

I feel the music of life playing all around me.
I hear the rhythm of life beating in my heart.
I sing out the happiness of who I am as my
soul harmonises with the rhythm of creation.

I am wisdom

The wisdom in me is specific to my journey.
I am aware of what I need to know and when
I am prepared to learn.
I am wise at all times, for my choices are
appropriate to my learning.
My wisdom is connected to the Creator of All
That Is.

I am mind

The navigation instrument of my soul's journey, my mind is representative of my soul's expression of purpose, purity and love.
The focus of my mind is to serve my soul.

I am soul

I am soul, therefore I am vision.
Therefore, I am all-knowing.
Therefore, I am connected to the Creator of All
That Is.
Therefore the best of what I am shines forth.

I am a master

In me is the knowledge I seek.
In me is the teacher I seek.
For I am the architect of my journey through
the landscape of the Divine Spirit.

I am spirit

I have chosen my time on Earth to fulfil my
desire to master compassion.
Through my service to others I express my
devotion.
Through my acceptance of the spirit, I am
compassion.

I am nature

I am the link between thought and action.
I am beauty within creation.
I am in communion with nature.
My role in nature is balance.

I am all colour

In me is the unconditional love of pink.
In me is the sensitivity of pale blue.
In me is the self-empowerment of maroon.
In me is the mind's wisdom of yellow.
In me is the nurturing of green.
In me is the communication of orange.
In me is the commonsense of brown.
In me is the balance of lilac.
In me is the awareness of purple.
In me is the balance of all life draped in Divine
white light.

I am creation

As I breathe, I connect to the breath of
creation.
As I observe, I see the wonder of creation.
As I feel, I sense creation all around me.
As I speak, I hear the advancement of
creation.
I am a pulse within creation.

I am

I am because I chose to be.
My soul, during a time of great wisdom and
learning, sought my life's path to evolve in
feelings.

I am my breath of life

As I breathe I am aware of life flowing
through me.
I open to Soul and Spirit with every breath
I take.
I expand my wholeness.
I am Soul.

I am advancement

My presence on Earth contributes to its progress.
From the moment of birth to the moment of death I advance reality, for I am an integral part of the Divine Plan.

I am an expression of all that is

I am Spirit.
I am Mind.
I am Soul.
I am everlasting life.

I am balance

My mind, body and soul live in harmony for my wellbeing and peace on Earth.

I am sensitive

I allow the needs of the world to flow through
me so that I can see clearly my contribution to
the world's reality.
I know that my thoughts and feelings
contribute to the world about me.

I care

In every way, in every day, I show the world I care.
My words and actions draw others to the light of the Divine spirit.
My words and actions light the path of my soul.

I am blessed

I am Spirit in flesh.
I have been given life so that I may grow
in love.
I increase my grace through devotion to my
evolvement.
In this way I serve the evolvement of
humankind.

I walk the path of unity

I am one with myself.
I am peace in myself.
Myself is whole.
I belong to others as they belong to me.
Separately we are many.
Together we are one.

affirmations
for
YOUR
LIFE

LIFESTYLE, WELLBEING AND RELATIONSHIPS

As we journey through life it presents us with all manner of issues and encounters which we must process in order to live another day. Good and joyful experiences aren't difficult to embrace. However, sadness, despair, fear, loss, ill health and misfortune seem, at times, to zap the willingness and energy to cope.

Motivation to change your reality may come from the oddest places. A beautiful young woman aged thirty had dated four middle-aged businessmen since she was nineteen years old. Each of the lengthy relationships presented as honest, open and sincere, and entertained the notion of marriage and children.

Nothing could have been further from the truth. All of her boyfriends turned out to be married men with children. She wondered how she could have made the same mistake four times.

Chancing on a women's magazine in a dental surgery, an article prompted her to take action and to turn her life around. She consulted me. I devised an affirmation that I thought would help to alter her psyche. For her part, she had to create a new and different reality in order to develop her new self. She traded glamourous clothes for a sophisticated casual style, so that when she looked into a mirror an immediate change was made obvious. Next, she focused on a less confronting and preying work environment. It was goodbye to the city job and welcome to a small family business in the suburbs. She stopped clubbing and cultivated new friends in interest groups: healthy cooking, dancing and calligraphy. Two years on, she met and fell in love with a local tradesman. For their honeymoon they spent one year touring and working around Australia. They have two children and a thriving small business.

I advise you to read through the affirmation that is relevant to you at this moment in time. Then devise what action to take. For instance, long-term unemployment action would be to search the job market or place your résumé on community notice boards. For health issues, the action is in understanding the illness and exploring all the avenues of successful healing.

Enjoy your journey of hope and healing.

Lifestyle

A New Year's resolution

The year will bring forth new beginnings.
Days of challenge and days of reward.
I am open to all learning.
For as I learn, I expand.

At any given moment I am me.
I can only be myself.

To look to the image of others is not me.
My aspiration is to be true to myself.

My love is endless.
It neither sees nor feels
the human barriers of jealousy,
envy or resentment.

My truth unfolds each day
to show the measure of my progress.
In Life I abound
with the fullness of achievement.

I know I am a soul
engaged in human experience.
Therefore it is my intention
to provide quality thoughts and deeds
to improve my life.

At peace with myself, I have true purpose.

Repeat this affirmation once daily for one week.

Attracting quality and abundance

Conceived in love,
I deserve quality of life.

Repeat each affirmation once daily for each week.

Having committed no crime against my fellow
nor traded my dignity for self-pity,
I deserve quality of life.

Being of even temper
and generally kind to all living things,
I deserve quality of life.

I deserve quality of life.
For I am a cog in the wheel of humankind,
creating the wholeness of living.

Being inspirational

I am a person of foresight.
I am a person of unlimited wisdom.

I delve into my reservoir of knowing
to release insightful direction.

Repeat this affirmation once daily for one week as required.

Challenging indecision

Thoughts flow freely through me supported by inspiration and insight.

My mind is flowing freely with clarity of thought.

Releasing talent

I believe in my creative ability.

I know I have something to offer.

I feel talent in every cell of my body.

I am resourceful in my creative expression.

Repeat this affirmation once daily for one week as required.

Promotion and recognition of work

My performance is that of
a conscientious employee.

My record is exemplary.

I am responsible, efficient and effective.

I deserve greater recognition of my skills
and contribution to the organisation.

Repeat as regularly as required.

Overcoming unemployment

I am of value to my community.

I am of value to industry.

I have qualities to offer the career
of my choice.

Repeat an affirmation each day, then repeat the cycle for
as long as required.

DAY TWO

I am willing to commit myself
to long-term employment.

I am open to learning
and to expanding my skills.

If change decrees an opportunity
for employment,
I am willing to alter my focus.

DAY THREE

I know I have left no stone unturned in my search for long-term employment.

I am satisfied with the effort I have made. I welcome new opportunities.

I am an honest, loyal and reliable person.
I am worth employing.

I know that the right job will find me eager
to give it all I've got.
I look forward to joining the workforce.

DAY FIVE

Reality is revealing its plan.
At the right moment in time
long-term employment will be mine.
I see myself content in my work.

Involuntary retrenchment

One door has closed so that
another can open.
If I am observant I will see my new direction.
I am secure in knowing I am of value
to the workplace.

I am open to learning in my new job.
I reject anxiety and worry.

Repeat affirmation daily for as long as required.

Creating a small business

I am filled with the inspiration to
create independence and success
through establishing
and managing my own business.

When prepared and adequately resourced
I can achieve what I desire.

Repeat each affirmation daily for each week.

Creative ideas are doing a merry dance in my head, pulling me to and fro through the ifs, buts and maybes of caution.

But when prepared and adequately resourced I can achieve what I desire.

I stop and think for a moment.

Have I done all the research I need to do?
Have I outlined all the flaws in my plans?
Have I prepared for that 'rainy day'?
Am I secure in myself?

I carefully evaluate my next step
To ensure my success.

I have in perspective my goals,
and know that the planned steps that I take
will secure my dream of successfully
conducting my own business.

Retirement

Life has entered a new phase.
One that is free of the hustle and the bustle of
the daily work routine.

I have a clean slate on which I can design
and plan whatever activities I choose.

I allow life to guide me to any necessary
changes to reach fulfilment.

My life is worthwhile.

Repeat each affirmation twice daily for three months.

Wellbeing

Self-confession for personal growth

I know I live a lie.
I pretend to be what I am not.
I pretend to have what I have not.
I create an outer image which does not reflect
the me that I know so well.
Therefore the people in my life don't know me
because I don't portray my true self.

I don't mean to deceive.
It's just my way of protecting and
compensating for what I perceive is not
acceptable in myself.

Perhaps my judgements are too harsh.
I should let life be my guide,
and reject the limitations of self-criticism.

Right now, I can feel the shift of change
in my emotional attachment
to the Lie I thought I was.

The healing has begun.
In my daily life I look for signs of
new-found strength of conviction.

With every minute of every day I evolve
beyond my self-restriction.
I know and realise that self-forgiveness is
the blessing of the soul.

Repeat affirmation daily for one week.

Affirming intuition

I know I am more than human.
More than flesh and blood.
More than thought and feeling.

I know I am inspiration itself,
abounding in the beauty and wholeness
of reality.

I am a gift to life
as life is the gift for me.

Repeat each affirmation once daily for each week.

I intuitively know to listen
to the inspiration of my mind,
the instinctive behaviour of my
emotions, and the sensitivity
of my physical body
throughout its daily pace of life.

I respond to life intuitively.

Each intuitive expression
serves to expand my consciousness.
I observe my intuition.

I am expanding intelligence.

All intelligence is at one
with intuitive expression.

I see examples of my intuition
at work each day.

Increased insight is expanding my awareness of the world around me.

My intuition has challenged my logical mind,
giving increased insight of my world.

I have faith in my intuition to lead me
through life.

Optimum health

My mind enjoys the clarity of clear thinking.
My body enjoys free flow
and unrestricted movement.

My emotions enjoy self-attunement
encompassing the world around me.

My spirit is graced with the blessing of life.

Repeat affirmation once daily on waking for as long as
needed.

Weight alteration

The image I see in the mirror does not
impress me.
I resolve to find a solution
to my disappointment.
I know that physical change requires
a change of attitude.
I am prepared to make the effort.

Repeat each affirmation in three-day cycles as long as
needed.

DAY TWO

I delve into self-questioning.

Why do I look the way I do?

How do I change in order to improve
my weight?

I am open to personal insight.

Solutions and skills flow through me.
I feel positive change altering my attitude,
which will bring my weight to my desired
balance over an appropriate period of time.

Overcoming fear

My mind has woven threads of restrictive fear
through my thoughts, emotions and body,
blocking my ability to respond
to inspiration and progress.

I shall use my mind as a tool of my soul
so that I do not become enslaved by fear.

Repeat each affirmation once daily for each week.

Although ensnared by threads of fear
in my mind,
I know the soul that I am can inspire
great things.
I challenge my restrictive fears to
be open to progressive change.

I use my mind as a tool of my soul so that I do
not become enslaved by fear.

WEEK THREE

My unhealthy fear turns to strength as
I challenge myself to recognise the fact and
fiction of my aspirations and anxieties.

I use my mind as a tool of my soul so that I do
not become enslaved by fear.

I challenge myself to rise beyond restrictive
fear with the clarity of self-recognition and
prophetic insight.

I use my mind as a tool of my soul so that I do
not become enslaved by fear.

Addictive behaviour

I walk free of my addiction.
I think free of my addiction.
I feel free of my addiction.
I act free of my addiction.
I am free of my addiction.

Repeat each affirmation daily for as long as required.

Stress relief

The tension that has invaded every cell of my body threatens to impair my wellbeing unless I make a firm commitment to do all within my power to change the stressful situation or adopt a different attitude to handling it.

I will make the stress work for me, not against me.

Repeat affirmations until the stress is alleviated.

I will make the stress work for me, not against me. I seek to learn and grow from the stress, not to be restricted by it. I resolve to respond to stress as an observer, not to react to it.

Pain management

I choose to exercise my willpower to help me cope with the pain that is disrupting my quality of life.

My mind has the power and the determination to rise above the pain.

I allow my body to heal free of pain. I allow my body to be free of pain.

Repeat affirmations twice daily for as long as required.

Cancer

I know that life has a special way of offering
hope when the chips are down. I implore hope
to come to me immediately.

Repeat each affirmation three times each day, then repeat
days six and seven for ongoing healing.

DAY TWO

I summon my survival instinct to provide the strength that I need to move forward in search of a solution.

DAY THREE

I resolve to move past the shock of being diagnosed with cancer, towards the modality of healing that will restore me to good health.

People all over the world are being cured of cancer by orthodox or natural methods.

Where there is hope there is joy.

Cancer is challenging my life and awakening every emotion, causing me to see and feel what I hold most dear.

It presents change and offers me two options:

1 – to reflect and renew my life fully in mind, body and spirit, releasing self-destructive patterns of lifestyle.

2 – to prepare my consciousness to transcend to the glory of death, where peace is offered to all who cross its threshold.

I welcome the opportunity of renewal.

I see my body and my life in a new light and
seek to understand them more fully.

DAY SEVEN

My journey of self-discovery has begun.
Though challenging, I welcome the
opportunity to evolve.

Preparing to die

As the end of my life approaches, I wish to make peace with myself and everyone who has touched my life.

I resolve my life with the absolution of truth.

Repeat an affirmation each day. In an emergency, repeat the third affirmation twice daily as long as required.

DAY TWO

I forgive myself for the things I didn't do. For the goals I didn't attain. For the dreams I didn't fulfil. I release all disappointment.

I resolve my life with the absolution of truth.

DAY THREE

I open myself to transition. I welcome a new beginning. I accept the blessing of pure love.

I release my life with the absolution of truth.

Relationships

Attracting a relationship

I believe I am worth loving. I am open to caring and sharing. I freely offer my devotion to the one who offers the same to me in return.

I look forward to opening my life to true love.

Repeat each affirmation once daily for each week.

I know that Fate is not fickle and that at the right moment in time my true love will cross my path.

I look forward to opening my life to true love.

My true love, my expectations are as follows:

You are my lover, my best friend, my soul mate. I trust you implicitly. I promise to hold you dear in my heart till death do us part. I will share the good times as I will life's difficult encounters.

Our love is a blessing of creation.

Fate at this very moment is unfolding the plan of our union. At the right moment in time, we will hold each other close. We will discover that this is the love we've been waiting for. We will realise we are meant to be together always. We will recognise each other's strengths and weaknesses.

As the spontaneous commitment of true love binds us, we will know that love's blessing has enriched our lives equally.

This affirmation course can be repeated every second month until fate brings your true love to you.

Turbulent relationship

(parent/child or partner)

Nothing is resolved through anger and aggression. Nothing is resolved through self-centredness or selfishness. Nothing is resolved through lack of compromise. Nothing is resolved through imposing restriction. Nothing is resolved by unrealistic expectations.

Communication begins with listening to what is being said and felt by the other person. A change in attitude can alleviate the tension. The conflict will be resolved amicably.

Repeat affirmation daily.

Divorce

Loving feelings that once were, have been eroded by time and circumstance.

Repeat this cycle of affirmations for as long as it takes to be released from the trauma of divorce.

The bitter emptiness that overshadows
my day-to-day existence serves as a grey
reminder of what has led me to divorce.

The joyful memories somehow got lost among the painful memories. Try as I may, resentment resides in me now.

When I am healed I will be able to look back on this period and see what it taught me. But at present I know I must grieve in order to be released from these taunting feelings.

I am moving past looking for someone to blame. Instead I look forward to the hope of a brighter tomorrow. I seek to enrich my life, not bury it in anger or self-pity.

Caring for aged parents

When I look into your eyes I see a life filled with memories. Yet your aged figure reflects little of who you have been to the many people who have crossed your path, including me.

At times I am saddened by your ageing, seeing the vibrance of life slipping away, while at the same time understanding the inevitability of it all.

I aspire to loving you as your offspring and caring for you as a nurturer. I know that I am now your life-line, as you were mine during childhood. Although at times I may waver or feel stifled, I have the strength of conviction to be here for you always.

Repeat affirmations daily as long as you need to.

Preparing for childbirth

I feel the love between us growing stronger each day of your development.

Our bodies are in complete harmony, giving and taking what is needed for a healthy union.

On the day you choose to be born, our bodies will synchronise each movement. Our thoughts will be as one.

As mother and child, we will work together to deliver you with ease into the world.

Repeat affirmations daily until delivery, placing both hands over the foetus.

Challenging childlessness

In moments of self-analysis, I wonder why I have no children. What seems so difficult for me to achieve seems so very easy for others.

Every time friends or family glow with contentment at the confirmation of their pregnancy, tears of frustration and loss filter into my eyes, behind closed doors I grieve.

I feel that my life plan has been drastically altered without my consent. I seek to overcome my childlessness.

Repeat each affirmation daily for each week. Then repeat weeks three and four regularly until conception.

I wonder…

Is a home a home without children? Is a relationship a family without children? Is my sexuality fully expressed without children? Am I complete without sharing the lives of children? Is marriage fruitful without children? What is there to life without children?

I need to harness my fear of childlessness and convert it into personal strength.

I feel the joy of prospective parenthood.
I dispel the fear of childlessness. I awake to
the challenge of creating a reality of life with
children.

I know that there are children waiting to be born unto me. I call on destiny to choose a moment of conception.

I am worthy of the care and love of children.

Loss of a baby

At times I wonder what it would be like to hold you in my arms again, to watch as you sleep, to hear you cry, or see you smile at me. Resentment and anger walk hand-in-hand and ask, 'Why?'

Grief seems such an empty word. It doesn't say how much I loved you. It doesn't say how much I miss you. It doesn't explain how much I cared. It doesn't even tell of the flesh and blood we shared.

The bond of love knows no eternal separation.

Repeat each affirmation twice daily for one week.
Week three can be repeated for as long as needed.

When I think of all the plans I had for us
I realise that my expectations have been
shattered.

Is it any wonder that I feel lost to sorrow?

The bond of love knows no eternal separation.

WEEK THREE

I release myself from the torment and guilt of grief so that I can heal my loss.

I know in my heart that divine love heals all.

The bond of love knows no separation.

To the unborn child

Though our parting has left a hollowness within, time will seal the gap.

I shall always treasure the moment we were one.

The evolution of your soul has been graced with a divine blessing.

Be at peace.

Mourning

I am hurting because I have loved you with every cell of my body. I mourn my loss openly and without shame I grieve our separation because you were an integral part of my life. I miss you so much.

The pool of emptiness that threatens to drown me with its tears is simply an expression of my love for you. It gently and slowly nourishes my loss, washing away fear and grief.

Memories live forever, people do not.

Repeat each affirmation daily for the week or weeks specified.

When time has healed my loss, I will be renewed, and equipped with the resilience of survival and the richness of the memories of you.

Memories live forever, people do not.

My sense of emptiness and disillusionment is because you are gone from my sight and touch. I find it difficult to believe I will never see you again. I release myself from this pain. I feel you in my heart and in my mind. I sense you are near. I know we will not be separated forever.

Memories live forever, people do not.

I know that death is merely a phase in the chain of life. My loved one lives on in me for he/she has touched my every cell, my very being and shown me love.

Memories are life's treasures.

WEEKS SEVEN AND EIGHT

The bond we shared lives on in my memories.
There we can never be separated.

Memories are life's treasures.

I am indeed fortunate to be blessed with the memory of you.

Suicidal death of a loved one

Did you realise when you took your own
life that I would be haunted by the question
'Why?'

Did you foresee the unknowing guilt that
challenges my mind as I wrestle with my
conscience each day?

Did you realise that in gaining your freedom
you imprisoned me in tortuous emotions?

And did you realise that the peace you sought
has brought me unrest?

Why didn't you know that I cared enough to be there for you? In good times and in bad?

Why didn't you know?

Although time may never answer my wondering, it will soften the hard edge of my despair.

Repeat affirmation once daily for the week or weeks as specified.

Questions march through my mind in relentless search for answers that don't want to be found.

Confusion and bewilderment are of no value to my healing.

I seek the quiet realm of knowing that you are now content and at peace.

I open myself to peace of mind and comfort of heart knowing that although time may never answer my wonderings, it will soften the hard edge of my despair.

In many different ways life challenges us all daily. Some people like myself are strong enough to bounce back. Others like you fear what tomorrow may bring.

I ask myself, who am I to condemn your fear?

I forgive you and I forgive myself.

Time is softening the hard edge of my despair.

Judith Collins is a renowned social ecologist, author and public speaker. With forty years of experience in healing, education and organic farming, she has become a regular on television and radio. In 1983, she was awarded the prestigious Advance Australia award in recognition for her contribution to the community. Judith lectures, writes for a number of magazines and conducts courses around Australia and internationally. She has recorded several guided meditations and two children's stories. Judith lives in the Southern Highlands, New South Wales.

judithcollins@earthkeepers.com.au
www.earthkeepers.com.au

Also by this author:
Companion Gardening in Australia